MY AMERICAN JOURNEY

From Ground to Air

with the Wright Brothers

BY DEBORAH HEDSTROM-PAGE

ILLUSTRATIONS BY SERGIO MARTINEZ

FROM GROUND TO AIR

ISBN: 978-0-8054-3273-2

Published by B&H Publishing Group
Nashville, Tennessee

Dewey Decimal Classification: F

Subject Heading: WRIGHT, WILBUR \ WRIGHT, ORVILLE \
FLIGHT—FICTION \ AIRPLANES—FICTION

1 2 3 4 5 6 7 8 9 10   11 10 09 08 07

Foreword   5

Introduction   7

CHAPTER ONE
Flying Fascination   11

CHAPTER TWO
Kitty Hawk Camping   14

CHAPTER THREE
Nosedive   19

CHAPTER FOUR
Tunnels and Tails   22

CHAPTER FIVE
Gliding on Air   27

CHAPTER SIX
The Race Is On   30

CHAPTER SEVEN
Collapsed, Broken, and Cracked   35

CHAPTER EIGHT
59-Second Success   38

EPILOGUE
The Sky's Not the Limit   42

Character Building: Patience   44

Activities   62

Foreword

It's no big deal to see an airplane today. Rockets even blast off to Mars! But a hundred and ten years ago people only dreamed of soaring in the sky.

Even though people's ability to fly is just over a century old, their desire to fly is ancient. For thousands of years people have dreamed of sailing through the air like a bird. Ancient Greeks told of Icarus, a boy who flew on wings made of feathers stuck together with wax. The great Italian painter Leonardo da Vinci filled notebooks with sketches of flying devices in the 1400s. And for centuries people jumped off cliffs and towers, flapping homemade wings or wearing capes like our modern superheroes in an effort to fly. Most ended up hurt or killed!

Finally, in 1783 François Pilâtre de Rozier got into a basket attached to an enormous balloon filled with heated air. It floated! For the first time ever, a person felt the stomach-lurching excitement of liftoff. For the first time someone looked down and saw people and animals grow smaller and smaller until they looked like ants scurrying along the ground.

But floating wasn't really flying. Could something heavier than air defy gravity and travel against the wind? Many people thought so and they kept trying to make airships with engines that would climb up and move through the air on their own.

By 1898 people had made small model planes with engines and even had ridden on gliders. But no one had felt the rush of powered flight. Then Wilbur and Orville Wright got interested in flying.

From Ground to Air with the Wright Brothers tells their story. From their first stomach flip-flop at liftoff to their thrilling ride through the sky, you'll be there. Joining you in this adventure will be a fictional thirteen-year-old named Becky Miller. She lives on Kitty Hawk Island, North Carolina, but spends the winters with her grandma in Dayton, Ohio. She desperately wants a job at the Wright Cycle Company, making and repairing bicycles.

As in all the other *My American Journey* books, Becky does not change the true history of the Wright brothers' race to fly the first powered airship. Each adult you meet, each piece of canvas you hear being sewed, and each nosediving swoop you watch—really happened. So check the sky and get ready for takeoff!

Introduction

Becky looked up into the sky and wanted to shout her good news. But instead she walked down the street, trying hard not to skip—after all she was thirteen years old. Then she spotted her friend, Franklin, and forgot that yelling wasn't too grown-up either. "I got a job fixing bicycles at the Wright Cycle Company!" she hollered. "Mr. Wilbur Wright himself hired me."

"No foolin'?" Franklin asked. "I guess for a girl, you are pretty good with tools."

Wrinkling her nose at her friend, Becky let the remark pass. Both of them knew her dad had taught her more about building and fixing things on Kitty Hawk Island than Franklin had ever learned in Dayton. Besides it was an old argument, and she had big news. "You'll never guess what I saw on a bench in the cycle shop—flying machine wings!"

Franklin looked at Becky to make sure she wasn't pulling his leg to get even for his crack about her being a girl. When he saw sheer excitement on her face, he realized the wings must be real and started rattling off questions. "What did they look like? Were they like the rocket's in this week's *Pluck and Luck* airship adventure?"

The bullet-shaped flying machine on the front cover of their favorite story magazine came to Becky's mind. "No, that had four propellers on each side of it with just small fins in front and back. The wings the Wright brothers are making look a little bit like bird wings. They're shaping them out of wood, and they have moveable parts."

"Do you think they'll fly?" Franklin asked.

"I don't know. These wings don't look anything like the airships in our adventure stories. But no matter what they look like, Granny will say the whole thing is tomfoolery."

The mention of Becky's grandma brought Franklin to a halt. Grabbing his friend's arm, he said, "You're not going to tell your grandma about the wings you saw, are you?"

Becky stopped suddenly and said, "Oh my gosh, I better not. She was reading about another crash just

this morning in the newspaper. A man in New Jersey broke his ribs when he tried to fly off a cliff. Rescuers found him bleeding and unconscious among the smashed remains of his flying machine."

After letting out a low whistle, Franklin said, "If a person gets hurt or dies in a flying-machine crash, your grandma sure finds out about it. I can't count how many times she's looked at one of my airship stories and said . . ."

Becky joined in and helped repeat her granny's favorite saying, "'If God had intended men to fly, He would have given them wings.'"

They laughed as they started walking again, but then Becky said, "You can't blame her. Most people in Dayton think the same way. Besides, it's not just the crashes. Nowadays someone is always trying to con people out of their money with some flying scheme."

Nodding in agreement, Franklin said, "I know. I saw an ad just yesterday by a convict in a New York prison. He said he had a flying craft that could travel three hundred miles per hour. He offered to sell it for twenty-five thousand dollars and a pardon."

"Well at least the Wright brothers are honest," Becky said. "The truth is, they don't want a whole lot of people to know what they're doing. I think they're afraid someone might steal their ideas."

"Maybe someone would," Franklin said. "A ton of people sure want to fly. I heard my dad say that the military paid some man at the Smithsonian to build an aeroplane for use in the Spanish-American War, but the war ended before he could get the thing to fly."

For a few more minutes Franklin asked questions, comparing the airship piloted to the moon by *Pluck and Luck's* daring hero and the one being built in the back of the Wright brothers' cycle shop. But then he remembered how important this job was to his friend. She came to Dayton every winter and stayed with her grandma because money was scarce for her family on Kitty Hawk after the fishing season ended. "Gee Becky, I got so excited about the wings, I forgot to ask about your new job."

"I didn't think I'd get it," she answered as she kicked a rock off the pavement. "Wilbur Wright kept looking at me funny and pausing when he asked questions. I began to think Tommy Whipple was right when he said the brothers weren't too comfortable around females. But then Mr. Wright said to me, 'Normally, I would hire a boy in the shop, but you remind me of my sister, Kate, when she was your age. I'll give you a try.'"

Unable to resist, Franklin said, "I guess it pays to be a girl once in a while."

Becky playfully punched her friend in the arm. Ignoring his theatrical display of being hurt, she added, "While you twiddle your thumbs after school this winter, I'll be fixing cycles and test riding the new St. Clairs, Van Cleves, and Wright Specials the Wrights build in their shop."

Franklin felt a surge of envy. "You mean you'll even get to ride the Wright brothers' expensive model, the Van Cleve? It costs more than forty dollars!"

"I know," Becky said with a grin. "I also get to write in the shop record when the brothers are busy."

Franklin started to say "yuk" about the writing part of the job but decided against risking another punch in the arm. Instead he asked more questions about the work Becky would be doing on cycles. Eventually he had to say good-bye and head for home.

A few minutes later Becky opened the front door of her granny's house. Her excited and worried thoughts bounced off each other as she tried to figure out what to say. *I got a job and can send money to my folks now! But what if I can't do the work? I get to see a flying machine built and maybe even watch it fly! But what if it crashes and the Wright brothers end up hurt— or dead?*

Becky's struggle with her thoughts ended when her granny poked her head out of the kitchen door. One glance at the questioning look on her grandma's face and Becky forgot all but her excitement. She skipped down the front hall and yelled, "I got the job! I got the job!"

—DAYTON, OHIO: NOVEMBER 1899

Chapter One
FLYING FASCINATION

Dayton, Ohio: May 1900

The Wright brothers are busy warping wings or something like that, so I finally get to write in the shop diary. Orville told me, "Just record what happens today."

Diary Entry: Mr. Cordy Ruse came to the shop.

Actually "came" isn't the right word. He clanged to the shop in an auto car! Though I'd only been working at the Wright Cycle Company for a few months, I'd heard all about Mr. Ruse, the brothers' friend who built Dayton's first automobile.

When he brought his auto to a stop outside the shop, it let off a loud bang, poofed out a big cloud of smoke, and wheezed to a dying halt. "Cordy's here," Wilbur said. "There's no missing that noisy contraption he built."

I was painting the frame of a Wright Special when the commotion took place. The noise startled me and I ended up with blue paint splattered on my shoe. While wiping it off, I looked up and saw Mr. Ruse walk in. He was wearing one of the long, white coats that auto drivers use to keep the dust off their clothes. He went right over and clapped Orville on the back. "What's this I hear about you and Wilbur building a flying machine?" he asked.

Diary Entry: The Wright brothers told Mr. Ruse about their flying machine. They also talked about internal combustion engines.

But I thought only auto cars and the Wrights' shop equipment ran on these combustion engines— not airships. *Pluck and Luck's* flying machines and even the crashed ones that Granny reads about run on steam or electric power.

Mr. Ruse must have wondered about this, too, because his forehead got all wrinkly as he listened to the brothers. Finally he said, "But the little models that Samuel Langley flew had steam engines."

Wilbur smoothed down the few hairs covering his bald spot before he answered. "We know about

Langley's models, but they were way too small to carry a person and had to be launched by a catapult. We also know about Hiram Maxim's full-size flying machine. But with its heavy steam engine, it weighed eight thousand pounds and could barely get a few feet off the ground. The internal combustion engine can be made much lighter."

Mr. Ruse shook his head. "I don't know. The Smithsonian thinks Langley is right and so does the government. They're paying him to build a large version of his models."

I dipped my brush into the can and started painting the cycle frame again while the men finished talking. When Mr. Ruse headed out the door, I heard Wilbur say, "Cordy, you really should tie a sheet under that auto of yours to catch the parts as they fall off."

Both men laughed, but as I listened to Mr. Ruse's car clanging down the street, I thought Wilbur's idea sounded like a good one!

As I painted, my mind kept picturing the brothers in their white starched shirts, flying in a winged version of Mr. Ruse's auto car. In my daydreams, it banged, coughed smoke, wheezed, and then started falling to the earth. *Oh Lord, they'll be killed,* I thought.

Diary Entry: After putting together three Van Cleves and a Wright Special, the brothers worked on making sections of the wings moveable so they can be tilted up or down. They say this will help control where they fly and they call it wing warping.

This whole wing warping stuff made me ask lots of questions. That's when I found out the brothers' first flying machine won't have any engine at all! "It's going to be a man-carrying glider," Orville told me. "It will fly on the wind, and we'll use it to learn how to control our flight. Later, we'll add an engine for power."

I was pumping air into the tires of one of the Van Cleves when I heard this, and my stomach did a flip-flop. Forget the flying auto car. Now the brothers were planning to put on these moveable wings and plunge off a cliff!

"Rebecca, are you all right?" Orville asked.

I stopped pumping up the tire and said, "Can a man really glide on air?"

"Have you ever heard of Otto Lilienthal?" he asked. After I shook my head no, he said, "Otto flew sixteen types of gliders more than two thousand times! Wilbur read all about it to me when I had typhoid fever in '96."

Totally surprised, I almost knocked over the Van Cleve. "You mean this Otto guy actually flapped wings like a bird and flew?"

"No and yes," he answered while setting aside a tire rim he'd just welded and wiping his hands on his heavy, blue apron. "Gliders have fixed wings, so you can't flap them, but when the wind rushes under their surface, a person can fly like a kite or soar as a bird does."

"Then why do people crash all the time?" I asked.

"Because they rush into the air without thinking," Wilbur said as he brought another cycle to me that needed air in its tires. "People just want to fly. They don't study how to build or control a flying machine. Most don't even figure out how to land it before they take off."

Studying? Figuring? Wasn't flying just a daring adventure? Surely you didn't need a lot of school stuff to be able to fly. If so, it's no wonder people crash. They probably hate textbooks. "It seems to me," I said, "that this man Otto should tell people what they need to know so others can fly without doing math."

The brothers looked at each other and hesitated. Then Wilbur said, "Lilienthal's last glider stalled in the air, fifty feet above the ground. He fell, suffering severe injuries, and died two days later in a hospital."

Diary Entry: Painted the frames of three Wright Specials. Pumped air into a lot of tires and test rode a Van Cleve.

When I rode the Van Cleve, I pedaled fast, hoping that the rush of air in my face would wipe away my thoughts about Otto Lilienthal. His story really shook me up. He even knew how to fly—or glide, as the brothers said—yet he crashed! Maybe Granny was right that people weren't meant to fly.

What if the Wright brothers, in spite of all their studying, end up in a hospital?

I shivered as I rode back to the shop, and it wasn't because of the cool spring air.

Chapter Two
KITTY HAWK CAMPING

Kitty Hawk Island: October 1900

Wilbur is going to do it! He's really going to fly—oops, I mean glide! Everyone is busy checking the gliding machine and the wind conditions, so I get to do the diary entries. And it's happening on my island too!

Diary Entry: Orville checked the wind meter (he calls it an anemometer), and the wind is blowing twenty-six miles per hour. Wilbur says that speed is perfect for a manned flight.

I could hardly believe it when I learned that wind made the Wright brothers pick my island! It all started when Wilbur got a letter from the National Weather Bureau, listing places where the wind normally blew at least thirteen miles an hour. "Don't you live on an island off the North Carolina coast?" Wilbur asked me when he looked up from the list.

"Yes, sir. It's called Kitty Hawk," I answered while putting a cycle chain over a St. Clair's sprocket wheel.

"According to the Weather Bureau," he said, "your island is one of the few windy and isolated places with sand dunes."

Wiping my greasy hands on a rag, I said, "They sure got that right!"

The brothers kept talking about the places listed in the Weather Bureau's letter. I heard things like, "Too populated. Reporters would broadcast every improvement we made," and "No sand. We need it to soften the blow if we crash."

Always they came back to Kitty Hawk, and by the end of the day I knew the Wright brothers were going to test their glider on my island! Franklin's face turned green with envy when I told him the news.

Diary Entry: Mr. Tate arrived at camp early this morning to help with liftoff.

Getting Mr. Tate was my idea. He does everything—farms, fishes, acts as postmaster and even our mayor. He came to mind when Orville said they'd need an extra man to help. The brothers ended up

staying in the Tates' extra room until they got the glider put together. Mrs. Tate even let Wilbur use her sewing machine to sew the wing fabric.

Folks on the island are friendly toward the brothers and watch them with interest, especially since getting a mainland newspaper that told about Count Zeppelin's airship. It said that the Count put hydrogen gas cells in his airship, causing it to be lighter than air. It floated four miles with five people! The newspaper picture showed a huge, sausage-shaped ship with propellers sticking out of it.

This news made me hurry through my chores every day, so I could run over to the Tates and help the brothers. One day I arrived and found the glider all put together. It sure looked different from the Zeppelin! It's more like a bird with a bunch of wings. It has upper and lower main wings and a smaller one near the front that they call a nosewing. Also the glider is heavier than air. So it doesn't float like the Zepplin; unless the wind holds it up, it drops!

Diary Entry: The glider is kite tested and ready for flight. Everyone is hoping it goes better than the first time Wilbur tried to fly.

When they flew the glider like a kite, they controlled the wings' moveable sections by attaching ropes to the wing-warping T-bar. They also attached ropes to the elevator handles that move the smaller nosewing up and down. These ropes allowed the brothers to make the glider turn, stay level, and land.

For the test flights, the Wrights moved out of the Tate house and pitched a tent at the edge of the dunes. First they tried to fly it off a tower and it crashed. As I mended a rip in the fabric, Wilbur told Orville, "Mr. Chanute was right. He said flying off a tower was an unnecessary hazard."

"Who's Mr. Chanute?" I asked, forgetting my manners about not interrupting.

"He's an authority on flying," Wilbur told me. He attached a splint to a cracked wing board and added, "Mr. Chanute gathers facts from everyone who makes good flight attempts. Earlier this year I sent him a letter asking advice, and he offered suggestions like the one about not using a tower. I thought he might be wrong but he wasn't."

After we finished repairing the glider, Wilbur decided to try flying it the next day. I rushed through my chores faster than ever and got to camp just as Mr. Tate and the two brothers started trotting down the sand, carrying the glider. All at once, it started to lift!

Wilbur pulled himself onto the body frame, and then Orville and Mr. Tate let go of each wing and eased out the tether ropes. Wilbur was in the air!

He lay facedown and got his feet on the T-bar that controlled the wing warp and grabbed the elevators to raise or lower the nosewing. I held my breath as he slowly drifted upward on the wind . . . five feet . . . ten feet . . . fifteen feet.

Suddenly the glider started bobbing. Wilbur clung to the controls as the wind bounced him around. "Let me down!" he yelled as the wings and nose took turns dipping one way and then another. Orville and Mr. Tate pulled on the tether ropes until the glider and Wilbur lightly bumped onto the sand.

We ran over to make sure Wilbur was all right. He looked a bit ruffled but got off the glider unhurt. Orville shook his head and said, "Why'd you come down just when things were getting interesting?"

Brushing sand off his slacks, he said, "I promised Pop I'd take care of myself."

Taking care meant more days of flying the glider like a kite without anyone riding on it. This time the brothers loaded chains onto the glider to see how it would sail carrying the weight of a man. Finally Orville said, "We can't learn any more without going back into the air ourselves."

Diary Entry: The same way as before, the men got the glider in the air with Wilbur on it.

This time Wilbur didn't yell for help! The nose of the glider did drop after rising a few feet, but Wilbur started working the elevators with his hands and the wing-warping sections with his feet and got it up again. He picked up speed and raced along with the wind. Then the glider nosedived again, but somehow Wilbur safely landed.

When he made it down, I started jumping up and down and clapping. Orville went over and slapped his brother on the back while Mr. Tate said, "Thought you'd break your fool neck, but a sea gull couldn't have made a better landing!"

Wilbur's cheeks were pink and a starched shirt-tail hung out of his trousers. "It was incredible," he said grabbing his brother's shoulder. "You see the sand rushing below you and it feels like you're riding the wind. I want to go up again."

As Orville asked questions about controlling the glider, Wilbur went back to his usual studious self. "The tilt on the wing edges is wrong. It needs to be down, not up."

Diary Entry: Wilbur made more glides during the rest of the day. Some lasted fifteen whole seconds and went four hundred feet! His landings got better too.

Wilbur was flying—just like Count Zeppelin and all the heroes in the adventure stories. Granny's wrong. Man can fly, I decided. Then another thought came to me. That's what Otto Lilienthal believed too. The unwanted memory wiped the smile off my face and slowed the excited beat of my heart.

Chapter Three
NOSEDIVE

Kitty Hawk, North Carolina: August 1901

Everything's gone wrong! One thing after another has troubled the Wright brothers on this second trip to Kitty Hawk. Now even Wilbur and Orville feel discouraged and maybe a little scared! I think that's why they want me to write in the journal today.

Diary Entry: Wilbur stopped riding the new, larger glider. The brothers went back to flying it as a kite loaded with sandbags. Wilbur's face looks a lot better.

I should have known the summer was doomed when the mosquitoes hit before the brothers even got their second glider put together. The pesky insects came in like a dark cloud. No amount of slapping got rid of the buzzing biters! I escaped them in my house, but Orville told me later that the hangar he and Wilbur built didn't keep them out. "We wrapped ourselves in blankets with only our noses showing," he said. "If we so much as poked out an arm, it came back covered in bites."

Orville even told about it when he took his turn writing in the diary. "There was no escape. They chewed clean through our underwear and socks. Lumps swelled up all over my body like hen's eggs."

Mr. Tate finally helped get rid of the mosquitoes by burning old tree stumps. The smoke made everyone cough, but it sure beat being lunch for insects! Finally the men could put the glider together.

Inspite of the mosquitoes, things looked promising. Mr. Chanute, the aeronautics guy Wilbur told me about last year, had sent a couple of extra men to help. Mr. Spratt helped out a lot. He also knows the name of every plant and animal, and he tells great jokes. The brothers don't like the other man too well. I heard Wilbur say Mr. Huffaker was lazy, and Orville commented that he "borrowed" stuff without asking.

Diary Entry: Even with sandbags on the glider, the brothers cannot control it very well. It wing-dips, nosedives, and even stalls.

The first stall happened right after the men finished putting together the glider. The brothers had made the wings bigger so it took less wind to get it off the ground. Wilbur got up in the air but not far. Right off he nosedived back into the sand. On the next flights, Wilbur kept wiggling back on the glider's body trying to keep the nose up.

After a while the glider got up, but Wilbur had to stretch for the hand controls like a little boy reaching for a cookie jar. Then the glider stalled! Wilbur strained to work the controls. Watching his brother struggling, Orville started yelling, "Scoot forward!" Mr. Spratt and Mr. Huffaker yelled, too, and I let go with my best baseball park scream.

Wilbur heard us and when he scooted forward, the nose came up and the glider came down! Luckily it thumped lightly on the sand, instead of splintering into a thousand pieces. But it really shook the brothers up. I heard Orville say, "This is precisely the fix Otto Lilienthal got into when he was killed."

I didn't sleep well that night. Every time I closed my eyes, I pictured Wilbur falling out of the sky. Finally I got up and wrote Franklin a letter. After telling about the crash, I tried to explain about controlling air flight. "It's a lot harder than the adventure stories make it. Once you're in the air, you've got to control the glider three ways. First you've got to keep it from doing nosedives or taildives. Then you've got to keep it from doing left or right wing-dips. And once you get it level, you've got to make it go in one direction. It's tricky, real tricky."

Diary Entry: The Wright brothers have made changes to the elevators, wings, and body ribs trying to fix the glider's problem. Mr. Chanute, who came to camp a week ago, is impressed with the improved glider. He especially likes the hip cradle.

The cradle is pretty nifty. The brothers attached wires from the wing-warping sections to a sling that's the hip cradle. They hoped that Wilbur could lie in the cradle and only have to shift his hips to regain control when the wings dipped. But he's not sure if it worked.

When Wilbur got into the air and turned the glider, he lost control but couldn't figure out why. He told Mr. Spratt, "When I'm trying to control the flying machine in the air, I get so busy working my hands, my feet, and my hips while looking for a soft place to land, that my idea of what actually happens is very hazy."

Hazy isn't the right word for what happened two days ago—frightening is more like it!

Wilbur got up great. The glider's nose and tail stayed level, allowing him to skim along close to the ground. Suddenly one of the wings dipped and caught the sand. The glider spun, hitting the ground again and again before crashing to a halt. The jolting ride and abrupt stop threw Wilbur out the front of the machine on his face.

I've never seen Orville run so fast! When I came hurrying up after him, the first thing I spotted was Wilbur crumpled up on the sand. Then I saw the blood!

Orville was kneeling beside his brother and kept saying, "Are you OK, Will? Is anything broken? Can you get up?"

Wilbur groaned, rolled over, and spat sand out of his mouth. He had a couple of cuts on his face which caused the blood I saw. He also got quite a few bruises, but he walked back to camp with a hand from Orville.

Nobody said much, but that's when I thought the brothers must have felt discouraged and a little scared. Later I heard Wilbur tell Orville, "Man won't fly for another thousand years."

Diary Entry: Mr. Chanute leaves tomorrow, and Mr. Spratt and Mr. Huffaker will soon go back home too. The Wright brothers are talking of heading back to Dayton before the month ends.

It will be a few months before I go to Granny's and return to work in the cycle shop. From the brothers' talk, I'm not sure if they'll be building a third flying machine when I get there. This makes me feel all mixed up inside. I don't want the Wrights to fail, but I don't want them to get killed either. If only real flying were as easy as in stories.

Chapter Four
TUNNELS AND TAILS

Dayton, Ohio: December 1901

Wilbur might have said it will take a thousand years to fly, but he and Orville are doing their best to prove the prediction wrong! Today they're doing wind experiments, figuring math, and writing down a zillion numbers. So I'm doing the diary.

Diary Entry: Charlie and I are getting caught up on the bicycle inventory. Everything got behind when Wilbur left to make some speeches about flying. Finished the Van Cleves. Today we start work on the St. Clairs. The Wrights help as they can, but flight testing keeps them busy.

When I first got back to the cycle company after coming to Granny's, I found a stranger and some weird stuff that made me scratch my head. The stranger turned out to be Charlie Taylor. The brothers had hired him to run the cycle shop while they were at Kitty Hawk last summer. As for the weird bicycle and six-foot box, they're for doing experiments that will improve their glider. I never realized you could learn so much about flying with your feet on the ground!

Charlie filled me in on what happened after the brothers came home so discouraged. "When Will and Orv got back from your island, everything was all gloom and doom," Charlie said while cutting a crossbar for a St. Clair. "But then a letter came from Mr. Chanute asking Wilbur to speak about flying at a highfalutin society of engineers."

I stopped sanding the rough end of the bar Charlie had cut and asked, "You mean Wilbur got up in front of a bunch of people and gave a speech?"

"Yep," Charlie answered as he marked off the length of a St. Clair crossbar. "Planning for the lecture, Will rethought every detail of last summer's flying attempts. That's when he found the mistake."

"Mistake?" I asked. "I was sure the brothers had corrected everything possible."

At first only the grating whine of the power cutter answered me, but then Charlie said, "Otto Lilienthal's figure for air pressure and his lift-and-drag tables are wrong. The brothers used them when they made the second glider, so the size and tilt of the wings were off." Suddenly he started chuckling. "Wilbur sure shook up those engineers when he said Lilienthal had goofed. I guess Chanute, Langley, and others are using Otto's figures and they argued with Wilbur. When he got home he started doing tests to prove Otto's error."

Diary Entry: Took wheel off handlebars of the St. Clair cycle that the brothers used for their first wind experiments.

That bicycle sure looked funny with its "winged" third wheel above the handlebars.

Watching Orville pedal it down the street made me think he was trying to prove that the Wright bicycles could go as fast as the new motor-powered cycles Franklin told me about. But after each ride, Orville would catch his breath and then start writing stuff in the diary. One day I just had to ask, "What are you doing?"

Orville looked up from his notes and started going on about airfoils, drag coefficients, lift, angles, and airflow. I guess I looked pretty confused because suddenly he stopped and said, "Do you understand?"

"Not really," I answered, shaking my head.

He tried again, pausing to think of easier words. "The wheel mounted above the handlebar is free to spin in the wind. We attached two metal plates to act as foils or stops. We figured their size, placement, and angle using Lilienthal's tables. If they were correct, when I rode down the street in the wind, the wheel should not have turned because of the wind pressing against the plates. But it does spin, so Lilienthal's numbers are wrong."

I watched Orville turn the "wing" plates a quarter of an inch and asked, "But how does that help you fly?"

Getting back on the bike for another run, he said, "Once we know what drags against the wind, we can build wings that don't. This should stop stall-outs and make the most of the wind's power."

Diary Entry: Today's wind tunnel experiments showed the best angle for using the wind's lifting power. Charlie and I finished cutting and sanding all the crossbars.

The wind tunnel takes the place of pedaling up and down the street. It's a six-foot box with a fan in one end. It even works better than the funny three-wheeled bike because the wind's speed can be controlled by the brothers making the box's fan go faster or slower. A glass window on top of the box allows them to watch a miniature wheel with wings spin in the fan's breezes.

When I told Franklin about the bike, the tunnel, and math figures, he sighed and said, "Sometimes trying to really fly just doesn't hold a candle to the adventure stories. Even your grandma's newspaper articles are more exciting than this testing stuff."

"Maybe now," I said, "but just wait. The brothers are building a third glider!"

Diary Entry: Work on the glider continues. Besides redoing the wings, Wilbur is sure the tail needs to be changed.

Seeing wings in the shop again gives me the tingles. The brothers will be going back to Kitty Hawk next summer, and this time Orville wants to try flying! I can just picture both brothers in the air. It will be like a *Pluck and Luck* adventure. I'm sure of it. It just has to be. It can't end in another crash.

Chapter Five
GLIDING ON AIR

Kitty Hawk, North Carolina: October 1902

The Wright brothers' new glider works great! The math stuff they did last fall and winter really paid off. The brothers are so busy flying—oops, I mean gliding—that I'm doing the diary today.

Diary Entry: Lorin chased two razorback hogs from the shed this morning. He also is helping Mr. Tate launch the glider.

Orville and Wilbur's brother, Lorin, came to the island. I guess their letters home got him interested in flying. Anyway he's real nice, and he even brought me a present from their sister, Kate. Handing it to me, he said, "I think she's happy you got Wilbur and Orville out of the house. When they left, she told me, 'Will spun the sewing machine by the hour while Orv squatted around marking the places to sew on yards and yards of canvas for the wings. There was no place in the house to live.'"

Kate's present resembled a small bear but it was soft like a pillow. "It's cute," I said, holding it in my arms, "But what is it?"

"I guess it's a toy or something," Lorin answered. "They're called *teddy bears* after a photo of President Teddy Roosevelt with a bear cub taken while he was hunting somewhere. People sure are buying them!"

While I sleep with my bear pillow, the Wrights sleep with hogs and mice. The hangar Orville and Wilbur built last summer was taken over by the animals during the winter. If the men aren't chasing the hogs, they're trying to whack the mice with a stick.

Diary Entry: Wilbur talked with Mr. Chanute and Mr. Spratt this morning. They wanted to know all about Orville's crash and the improvements made to the glider's tail.

The crash sure sucked the air out of me. Orville had only begun to fly and didn't know how to use the controls as well as Wilbur. But his gliding was going so well that none of us expected what happened.

Orville stalled in the air! The tail dropped, sending the glider straight down to the sand. When it hit the ground tail first, I heard a zillion loud pops and cracks as the wooden frame shattered into pieces. Canvas whopped in the wind and I froze. I wanted to scream and run, but instead I could only stare at the pile of broken boards and shredded canvas. Then Wilbur ran by me, hollering "Orville! Orville!"

His shouts jerked me out of my terrified daze, and I ran after him. We found Orville sitting in the middle of the wreck. No blood. No twisted body parts—just sitting. He looked at Wilbur and said, "I shifted the hip cradle to move the wings and forgot the elevator."

"Are you hurt?" Wilbur asked.

"I don't have a scratch or bruise on me, but the flying machine's a heap of cloth and sticks."

It took a week to fix the glider, and the whole time Wilbur kept talking about the tail rudder. "I don't know if it had anything to do with Orville's crash, but I've felt the glider lose control and skid when I've been in the air," Wilbur said. "I think we need to make the tail moveable."

Putting hinges on the tail's rudder and attaching wires from it to the moveable wing sections was a good idea; now the glider works even better. Each day the brothers improved their flying too. I can see why Mr. Chanute asks about their changes, but I don't think he understands the brothers' theories any more than I do. When Wilbur explained how the moveable rudder stopped the drag created by wing-warp, Mr. Chanute just sort of nodded his head and looked blank.

Diary Entry: Wilbur flew 75 times today and Orville flew 50! Once Wilbur traveled 662 feet and stayed in the air 62 whole seconds! They broke all kinds of records: largest flying machine used in any kind of weather; longest glide in America; longest time in the air; and gliding in the highest wind.

Wilbur flies the glider even better than Jack Wright flies his electronic air schooner in the newest *Pluck and Luck* adventure story. I wonder why the guy who wrote the story named his hero Wright. Maybe he's heard of Wilbur and Orville's flying.

Watching either brother fly makes me want to do it. They soar around like a big eagle and then drift down to a running stop on the sand. Yet on the day Wilbur took the glider up in thirty-mile-an-hour winds, I couldn't help remembering Orville's crash and I went all cold inside. I sure felt better when he came back down.

Diary Entry: Checked Orville's mousetrap and found it empty.

28

Orville isn't going to be happy when he hears this mouse is still on the loose. He spent half a day building a deathtrap for the critter, only to have the mouse scamper over his face last night and wake him up. "I've sworn vengeance on the little fellow for this boldness and insult," he told me when I got to camp yesterday.

Wilbur smiled the whole time his brother talked, so I guess it's all right that I hope the mouse doesn't get caught.

Diary Entry: Orville and Wilbur talked about adding a combustion engine when they get home to Dayton.

Hearing them talk about adding the engine made my heart start thumping. I can't get the smashed glider out of my mind. I know Orville walked away unhurt, but what if he'd been zooming through the air, powered by an engine instead of just gliding?

Well, Jack Wright flew an engine-powered airship in *The Mystery of the Magic Mine*. I know it's just a story, but surely the real Wrights can do as well as the imaginary one. At least I sure hope so!

Chapter Six
THE RACE IS ON

Dayton, Ohio: July 1903

A person just can't drop an engine in an airship and soar off into the sky. It takes a lot of planning, figuring, and inventing to hook it up to the right parts. But the Wright brothers are racing against others who are working on powered flight, so today they asked me to do the diary.

Diary Entry: Charlie Taylor and the brothers are rebuilding the internal combustion engine. Last month a gasoline leak froze the bearings and broke the crankcase. I worked on two Wright Specials.

When I left Kitty Hawk and returned to the cycle shop, right off Charlie warned, "The fur has been flying around here." Pointing at a bunch of drawings and fan blades, he continued, "Trying to figure out what propeller to attach to the flying machine's engine has Will and Orv shouting at each other something fierce."

"No, not the Wright brothers!" I said. My stomach felt like I'd just been punched.

I must have looked like I felt because Charlie quickly went on to say, "I don't think they're really mad. It's just their way of working through the problem. Why, half the time they convince each other they're right. Then Will starts arguing for Orv's idea while Orv starts arguing for Will's."

After hearing a couple of hot fights, I worried that Charlie might be wrong about the brothers' anger being authentic. Both of them were so fierce when defending their ideas. But once they've decided on a plan, they act as if a cross word has never been said. It must be a brother thing.

Diary Entry: A letter came from Mr. Chanute today requesting that Wilbur write an article about the wind-tunnel tests. He also says a man named Wilhelm Kress, as well as Mr. Langley, is trying to be the first person to successfully fly a powered airship.

When Wilbur read that Kress had joined the air race, he put the letter on the workbench and turned

to Orville. "Chanute wants me to write up our experiments, but I think I'll wait. If we make our information public now, it could help others carry off the prize from us."

This race to fly the first powered airship has Wilbur on edge. It all started a couple of years ago when Mr. Chanute told the brothers that the city of St. Louis planned an aeronautical exhibition to celebrate the hundred-year anniversary of the Louisiana Purchase. A big cash prize would be awarded to the first powered flier. For a while the race didn't bother the Wrights, but now a bunch of people are scrambling to fly first. As the date gets closer, the pressure increases.

Races and prize money are a big deal these days. Just this morning Granny glanced up from the newspaper and said, "Rebecca, listen to this: 'A cycle race is to be held this July in France. It will be called the Tour de France and cover 1,500 miles.'"

A picture of huffing and puffing cyclists came to mind. Having handled my share of steel frames, I knew bicycles weighed a lot. Pedaling one of them up and down hills for hundreds of miles sure wouldn't be easy!

But it's not just cycle and flying-machine races. Franklin keeps telling me about auto-car races too. "Henry Ford is the man to watch," he told me one Saturday while we pitched pennies. "He's won the Detroit Driving Club Race and the Manufacturer's Challenge Cup Race. His newest race car is called 'The Devil's Car.'"

As I flipped a penny at the brick wall of Franklin's house, I thought of Mr. Ruse's clanging and wheezing automobile. "They must go a whole five miles an hour," I said, feeling doubtful about the whole idea of auto racing.

"Are you kidding?" Franklin said. "This year's speed record is sixty miles per hour, and I'll bet you all my pennies that Ford breaks the record next year!"

I didn't take my friend's bet. If I put my pennies on anything, it would be on the Wright brothers in the air, not on Henry Ford on the ground.

Diary Entry: Charlie finished recasting another crankcase.

Having Charlie in the bicycle shop sure saved the brothers. No engine makers would build one like the Wrights wanted. When Wilbur got back from talking with the last manufacturer, he looked really glum. Orville asked him, "I take it this one said no too?"

Wilbur nodded as he walked over to the propeller and ran a hand down one of its blades. His silence bothered me, and I looked up from greasing a cycle chain. "Why don't you guys build one yourselves?" I asked.

Orville smiled but said, "We don't have—"

"Wait a minute, Orv," Wilbur interrupted. "Maybe we could."

Orville and even Charlie looked at him like he'd lost his mind, but he kept on. "Orv, you and I built the small combustion engine that runs the tube cutter and the welder in the shop. And Charlie is a top machinist who's worked on a lot of combustion engines. I think we can do it."

It didn't take much convincing before all three men were talking about blocks, pistons, cranks, and cylinders. I went back to the bicycle chain— something I could understand!

Spinning the wheel to make sure oil coated each link, I began to have second thoughts about my "helpful" idea. *What if the homemade engine failed? What if it conked out while in the air? What if it caused one of the brothers to crash?*

Chapter Seven
BENT, BROKEN, AND CRACKED

Kitty Hawk, North Carolina: December 14, 1903

The Wright brothers flipped a coin when they got here and Wilbur won. He's supposed to fly first, but it's been one repair after another ever since the brothers arrived in September. While they work, I'm doing the writing, so I haven't left for Granny's yet.

Diary Entry: Wilbur and Orville repaired left wing tip. Engine still runs fine.

That's a miracle. From the first time the brothers started the engine, it's had problems. Right off it rattled and shook so hard, it bent the propeller shafts. Boy, did that cause a delay!

We don't have machine equipment on the island, so the propeller had to be shipped back to Dayton where Charlie could fix it. The brothers didn't wait well. They fiddled with everything on the airship. It got so bad that one day I found Orville studying a book I couldn't read. "What's that?" I asked.

"I'm learning German," he said. He looked up from the pages and stared at the flying machine. "I'm also working on my French. I've got to do something to take my mind off flying."

When the propeller was finally returned, the brothers tested it to see how fast the engine could make it spin. It whirled around just great, but then Wilbur spotted a crack in the propeller. Once again it had to return to Dayton. "I'd better take it back this time," Orville said. "The shafts need to be made special with spring steel."

After Wilbur and I waited forever, Orville came back with the repaired propeller, and the brothers got all set to fly.

Diary Entry: Launch rails must be moved off Kill Devil Hill since they caused the crash.

Using the big dune called Kill Devil Hill had worried me right from the start. I'd seen some of my friends break their arms and legs sliding down its steep slopes on boards and paper sacks. But

Wilbur thought the added speed would help with takeoff.

The hill definitely got the flying machine going fast—too fast. Orville was running alongside to steady the airship on the rails, and he couldn't keep up. Suddenly the machine shot up at a sharp angle, slowed, stopped in midair, and fell back on the sand, flopping over to one side.

It all happened so fast, Wilbur landed in a daze. Though unhurt, he stayed on the tilted airship and didn't shut off the engine for a few seconds. When he stood up, even his slacks, starched white shirt, and tie didn't look too messed up. However, we all knew

he got off lucky. We remembered how Samuel Langley's pilot had almost frozen to death when the launch of his airship failed. It was launched off rails attached to a flatboat that was floating on the Potomac River. The first time it was tried, the powered airship dived straight into the water.

We learned about the pilot's second try when Orville got back from fixing the propeller shaft. He told us, "I read about it on the train to North Carolina. Langley and his people thought the first flight failed because of its launching machinery. So they worked on it and tried again a couple of days ago."

Orville shook his head in wonder as he started telling about the goof-up. "The airship took another dive! It went right off the end of the rails, only this time it flipped over and landed on its back in the freezing water. The pilot's clothes were caught on some of the wreckage until he finally managed to get loose. But then he was trapped under the water by ice. By the time he swam out from under it and was hauled back onto the boat, he was shivering uncontrollably. Others had to cut his clothes off of him."

It made me shiver just hearing Orville tell the story!

Diary Entry: While Mr. Tate and Orville move the rails, Wilbur's fixing the elevator support that broke when he crashed.

It feels like the brothers have been repairing their airship forever. But at least it's been repairable. Langley's flying machine was wrecked and his wasn't the first one this year. Granny sent me a clipping about another one. It read, "Wilhelm Kress attempted to launch his double-winged, engine-powered flying boat off the Tullernach Reservoir outside of Vienna. Unable to get into the air, the craft capsized and sank. Kress escaped without injury."

Reading and hearing about all these crashes sure makes me glad that Wilbur will be flying over sand. But I can't forget his wild ride off Kill Devil Hill, and I've got a big knot in my stomach. Soon the brothers will try to fly again. The first day the weather gets better, I know Orville and Mr. Tate will be running Wilbur and the airship down the rails again.

They'll be on level ground this time, but I'm sure glad that the men from the Kill Devil Lifesaving Station will be there. I just hope they don't have to do any lifesaving!

Chapter Eight
59-SECOND SUCCESS

Kitty Hawk, North Carolina: December 17, 1903

After three days of waiting for good weather, the Wright brothers are flying today. They have their hands full with the airship. I only have the diary and a pencil in mine but they're trembling. I'm to record everything as it happens.

Diary Entry: Dark clouds fill the sky. Sheets of ice cover the rain puddles on the dunes. The anemometer says the wind's blowing between 20 and 25 miles an hour.

It scares me that the Wrights are flying in this weather. They've never done it before when the sky looked threatening and the wind was blowing so hard. Even Mr. Tate didn't come to camp. I'm sure he thought the brothers would wait for better conditions.

But they're going ahead. This morning Wilbur said, "The weather is poor but winter is on us. It's now or never."

Diary Entry: Orville ran up the red flag to signal the Kill Devil Lifesaving Station that he and Wilbur would be test flying. Five men from the station arrived to watch.

I feel better with the rescue men here. But Wilbur wouldn't let them help with the flying machine. He said that unless a person is trained, one should not touch an airship. But since Mr. Tate isn't here to help him balance the wings, Orville must take off on his own.

First the weather and now no help with the launch!

Diary Entry: It's Orville's turn to fly. The brothers got the glider onto the sixty-foot launch track, and Orville fired the engine. Twice he got up, for 12 and 15 seconds. Wilbur made it once. The short flights prove the ship can take off but not much more. Wilbur is trying again.

I know the brothers want more than a short flight. But when Wilbur got his hips in the cradle and his feet on the T-bar, the wind pelted his face with grains of sand. Listening to the engine sputter and cough, I also saw how the wind rocked the glider back and forth on the launch rails. Wilbur looked

into the sky. Nothing. Even the sea gulls were staying out of the wind!

At least the short flights didn't get up into the worst of the wind gusts. Will the glider hold together if it gets up high?

Diary Entry: Wilbur nodded at Orville and pulled free the wire holding back the airship. Instantly it shot forward and rose off the tracks. It's not coming down! A station man named Mr. Daniels is taking photographs.

Oh no! The wind is knocking the airship around like a punching bag. Wilbur is frantically working his hands, feet, and hips, trying to correct each lunge in the wind.

It's nosediving. If I could only close my eyes. Orville and the station men are rushing forward. I put my hand over my mouth to choke off a scream. Wilbur zooms closer and closer to the sand. I can't hear anything—the crashing waves, the howling wind—I can only watch.

Diary Entry: A few feet from the ground Wilbur got control of the airship and eased it back up in the air. After only a short, bucking ride, he passed some invisible line in the sky where the wind smoothed out. He stopped darting and lunging and flew straight.

Orville started yelling and waving his arms and then the station men joined in. It took me a few seconds to realize they were cheering. Wilbur's flying! He's not gliding, but really and truly flying in a powered airship. I dropped the diary and started jumping up and down, waving my arms. "You did it! You did it!" I yelled.

Diary Entry: According to the stopwatch and propeller revolution counter started at takeoff, Wilbur flew for 59 seconds, going 852 feet. Needed repairs make more flights impossible today.

Needed repairs is putting it lightly, but this time the damage wasn't caused by the landing! Coming down in the wind, the airship did start bucking again. But Wilbur got it safely on the sand, only breaking an elevator on the nosewing.

After handshakes and pictures, the men carried the glider back to camp so the brothers could repair it and do another flight. At least that was the plan, but things didn't happen that way. Right after the men set the airship down, a fierce gust of wind caught one of its wing. Mr. Daniels jumped up and grabbed a handhold, but the wind was too strong. The glider rolled over and over, taking Mr. Daniels with it. By the time the brothers and other men finally got it stopped,

the aircraft was a broken jumble of wood, wire, and cloth. Mr. Daniels didn't get hurt, but it's going to take a lot more than one day to repair all the cracks, breaks, and rips in the airship.

Diary Entry: Message telegraphed to mainland telling of flying success. It read:

"Success. Four flights Thursday morning, all against twenty-one-mile wind. Started from level with engine power alone. Average speed through air: thirty-one miles. Longest 57 seconds. Inform press. Home Christmas. Orville Wright."

The Wright brothers flew the first, heavier-than-air, engine-powered flying machine in the world! Flying isn't just fiction any more—it's real.

Wilbur and Orville Wright's figuring, testing, and planning worked! Thanks to them, my granny now has a flying-success article to read, not another crash account. Now she's going to have to change her favorite saying to:

"If God did not intend for man to fly, He would not have given him a brain."

Epiloque
THE SKY'S NOT THE LIMIT

Bealeton, Virginia: February 28, 1927

Dear Franklin,

I finally tracked you down. I should have known you'd be in Highland Park, Michigan, working in one of Henry Ford's automobile factories! I looked for you because I want you to come to *The Flying Circus Aerodrome* in Detroit on May 1—you'll get to see me fly an aeroplane!

I figure of all the people I've shocked by following up on what Orville and Wilbur Wright invented, you'd understand the best. I got my flying license a few years ago. Actually I wasn't the first woman to do so. Harriet Quimby was. She got her license in 1912—just five years after the Wright brothers finally got a patent on their flying machine! She went on to be the first woman to pilot a plane across the English Channel.

Even a black woman named Bessie Coleman has hers. She couldn't get it in the United States because the flight schools refused to let her in due to her being a Negro and all. But that didn't stop "Brave Bessie," as we call her.

She went to Europe and got some French and German fliers to teach her. She started doing airshows to raise money for a flying school that would be open to all. It really upset me when I heard she died last year. She was riding with a test pilot, who nosedived and flipped the plane. Bessie fell out and plunged over five thousand feet to the ground.

Flying is risky, especially since the best way to earn money is by doing stunts in airshows. The Wrights had to do shows to support their work with airships for a while before the government started buying planes during World War I.

But death isn't limited to the skies. Wilbur died of typhoid in 1912 while the Wright brothers were fighting legal battles to get patents on their plane. You wouldn't believe how many men claimed that the brothers took their ideas. But the diaries we kept proved otherwise!

Granny went with me to Wilbur's funeral. I'm not much of a crier, but all my memories of starched white shirts, math figures, and flying tests made it so sad I just couldn't hold back my tears.

It was shortly after the funeral that I began to think seriously about flying. I thought Granny would have a heart attack when I told her, but she fooled me. For all her talk of crashes, she just said, "If you're determined to fly, learn how to do it right. I don't want to read no headlines about you crashing."

Speaking of crashes, we almost lost Orville in a bad one. He was demonstrating flight to the army for a big contract. After days of flying for more than an hour at a time, one of the plane's propellers cracked and the aircraft nosedived. Orville broke his left thigh and some ribs and ended up in a hospital for seven weeks! He walked with a cane for a long time but eight months after the crash, he went back to flying. Now he enjoys the freedom to concentrate on doing research, which he's good at!

Research is changing flying. The sky is no longer the limit. The latest advances have produced airplanes that can do amazing things. Charles Lindbergh is even planning a flight across the Atlantic Ocean this spring. Also we aviatrixes (as women aviators are called) are talking of forming a club called the Ninety-Nines. If we actually do it, I have little doubt that Amelia Earhart will be elected club president.

Sometimes it seems like a lifetime ago that I painted cycle frames, test-rode bikes and wrote in the Wright brothers' diary while they tested their gliders and flying machines on Kitty Hawk. It would be great to talk with you about old times— to laugh about the *Pluck and Luck* stories we read and our worries about whether real flight was possible.

Wilbur and Orville Wright ended those worries. They turned storybook flying into reality, and I've named one of my stunts the Wright Special. I sure hope you can come see it.

Your longtime friend,
Becky

Patience

Character Building with the Wright Brothers

Patience:

Mastering the Waiting Game

Anyone who has ever waited for Christmas morning, a birthday, or summer vacation knows that being patient isn't easy! And being patient isn't just waiting for things. Patience is needed whenever an event, person, or skill doesn't happen in the way you expect or want. Many people think that being patient means sitting and waiting calmly.

But being patient means more than sitting; it means doing what needs to be done. It's finishing your schoolwork while waiting for summer. It's playing a video game over and over even when you lose. Being patient also means getting excited and/or discouraged. If you're so eager for something to happen that you're discouraged when it doesn't, you need patience to wait for it.

The Wright brothers in our book *From Ground to Air* had a lot of patience—otherwise they would have ended up crashing like many other would-be fliers! Wilbur and Orville didn't just jump into making an engine-powered plane. Instead they gathered information, practiced with kite-type gliders, studied the currents in their wind tunnel, and built their own engine.

Patience allowed the Wright brothers to do what needed to be done even when they were excited and later discouraged about flying. Patience helped them succeed where others had failed. So let's take another look at their story and put it together with what the Bible and others say about patience.

Flying Fascination

Patience is not passive:
on the contrary it is active;
it is concentrated strength.
EDWARD BULWER-LYTTON

1. The Wright brothers wanted to fly. But instead of immediately trying to do so, they studied the flight efforts of other men. Name three other flyers they studied.

_____

_____

An impatient person often looks at other people's mistakes and dismisses them. But a patient person takes the extra time to think: What went wrong? How can it be improved?

2. In chapter one Wilbur says that flyers often crashed because they weren't patient. In their excitement to fly, they didn't figure out three things. Write down those three things.

_____

_____

_____

STUCK? *Look back on page 13.*

WHAT THE BIBLE SAYS

Read Hebrews 6:13–15
God made a promise to Abraham, . . .
"I will most certainly bless you, and I will greatly multiply you."
And so, after waiting patiently,
Abraham obtained the promise.

Read Genesis 12:1–4 and 21:1–5. How many years did Abraham have to wait to have a son? Now glance through chapters 13–20. Did Abraham sit and wait calmly for the Lord's answer?

_____

_____

IT'S YOUR TURN

Make a list of things that you are waiting for. They can be things such as your birthday, making a goal in soccer, or finding a close friend. Put a star by the one that is the hardest to wait for. Talk to God about it.

_____

_____

_____

_____

_____

CHAPTER TWO

Kitty Hawk Camping

Be patient in the little things. Learn to bear the everyday trials and annoyances of life quietly and calmly, and then when unforeseen trouble or calamity comes, your strength will not forsake you.

W. S. PLUMER

1. The Wright brothers did more than work on their glider. They also checked things that could affect flying. Write down one thing they did to prepare for their first flight.

_____

_____

If you've written to a government agency, you know it can take a while to get an answer. But the brothers waited for the Weather Bureau's letter, knowing it was vital to their success.

2. What happened when Wilbur tried to fly on the brothers' first glider?

_____

_____

3. What was Wilbur's response to his near crash?

_____

_____

STUCK? *Listen for the clank of chains and look back on page 17.*

WHAT THE BIBLE SAYS

Read Lamentations 3:25–26
The LORD is good to those who wait for Him,
to the person who seeks Him.
It is good to wait quietly
for deliverance from the LORD.

Reread this verse. Does God think it's bad to have to wait for something? What does He think about waiting?

_____

_____

IT'S YOUR TURN

Go back and look at the list you made in the last chapter. Do you think it's bad to have to wait for the things on your list? Can you think of any reasons that it might be good to wait? Talk to God about your thoughts. Ask Him to help you see some good in having to wait.

_____

_____

_____

_____

CHAPTER THREE

Nosedive

Patience is bitter, but its fruit is sweet.

JEAN-JACQUES ROUSSEAU

1. In chapter three the Wright brothers almost lost their patience and gave up. Write down what caused Wilbur's two crashes.

_____

_____

_____

_____

It will help if you remember the three ways that Wilbur had to control the glider.

2. Wilbur was pretty discouraged after his last crash and the hard time he had controlling the glider. What did he tell his brother before they left Kitty Hawk?

_____

_____

STUCK? *Wilbur was mistaken by 998 years!*

WHAT THE BIBLE SAYS

Read Romans 12:12
Rejoice in hope,
be patient in affliction;
be persistent in prayer.

Lots of times we think we have to wait for things because that's just the way it is. But according to this verse, who plans everything in our lives? Look at your answer. Whom should we talk to when it is hard to be patient?

_____

_____

IT'S YOUR TURN

Look at your list of things you must wait for. Write down how God controls each one. If you can't see how God fits into something, talk to Him about it. If you still can't see God in your waiting, talk to your parents or Sunday school teacher. You might not get a "perfect" answer, but you'll get some ideas to think about.

_____

_____

_____

_____

_____

CHAPTER FOUR

Tunnels and Tails

*There is no great achievement
that is not the result of patient working and waiting.*

JOHN HOLLAND

1. The crashes and other discouragements in chapter three eventually got the Wright brothers to run some tests and find out what was wrong. Write down two of the tests they did.

_____

_____

In 1901 companies didn't have fancy laboratories with expensive equipment. The Wright brothers made do in some pretty creative ways!

2. It wasn't enough to ride the windfoil bike down the street once or to try one shape of wings in the wind tunnel. Over and over the brothers had to do the tests, taking down each result. What do you think was required to keep doing the tests over and over?

_____

STUCK? *Sometimes the answer is right under your nose. Look back on page 25.*

3. Wilbur's and Orville's patience in running test after test eventually solved some basic flight problems. In the end, what did the brothers decide to build again?

_____

WHAT THE BIBLE SAYS

Read Romans 5:3–4
We also rejoice in our afflictions,
because we know that affliction produces endurance,
endurance produces proven character,
and proven character produces hope.

According to these verses, the things in our lives that require patience are good for us. What are some of the things that they develop in us?

_____

_____

IT'S YOUR TURN

Write down a few ways that you think patience can help you in your life—at school, with friends, with your brothers and sisters, or with your parents.

_____

_____

_____

_____

Gliding on Air

To know how to wait is the great secret of success.

J. M. DEMAISTRE

1. Learning how to fly also meant making mistakes. What big one did Orville make?

_____

_____

2. It wasn't enough to make a glider that flew, Wilbur and Orville also had to learn how to fly it! Over and over they went up into the air. How many times did the brothers fly the glider in one day?

Wilbur:_____

Orville:_____

If you need help, look back on page 28.

3. Again the brothers' patience in repeatedly flying led to finding and solving a problem. What did they improve on the plane?

_____

STUCK? *If the nose didn't dive and the wings didn't tip, what else on the plane could go out of control?*

WHAT THE BIBLE SAYS

Read Colossians 1:11
May you be strengthened with all power,
according to His glorious might,
for all endurance and patience, with joy.

It is easy for a person to say, "You need to have patience," but it is hard to stay calm and keep working when you want or need something. According to this verse, who can give you the strength to be patient? And is it OK to pray for patience?

_____

_____

IT'S YOUR TURN

Again look at your list of things that you have to wait for. Take some time and pray, asking God to give you the strength to be patient and wait.

_____

_____

_____

_____

CHAPTER SIX

The Race Is On

*There is no road too long
to the man who advances deliberately and without
undue haste; no honors too distant
to the man who prepares himself for them with patience.*
JEAN DE LA BRUYÈRE

1. Though the Wright brothers had patience, they blew it sometimes. As they worked on figuring out problems, what happened in the shop that showed the brothers lost patience at times?

_____

_____

When you lose patience with somebody, what often happens?

2. Though the brothers argued, how do we know that patience won out in their relationship and work?

_____

_____

STUCK? *If you need help, look back and read how their fights ended.*

3. Because the brothers and their friend Charlie had patience and were able to work through problems, what big job did they decide to tackle?

_____

WHAT THE BIBLE SAYS

Read Proverbs 15:18
A hot-tempered man stirs up conflict,
but a man slow to anger calms strife.

Sometimes it's hard to have patience with people. Your parents "lecture" too much. Your little brother gets into your stuff. And your friend can't make a basket. But this verse in the Bible says patience can help, even when dealing with people. How?

_____

_____

_____

_____

IT'S YOUR TURN

Think of someone you often lose patience and argue with. Think back. What is one thing that caused a lot of the fights? Ask God to help you have patience in this area. If you blow it, ask for forgiveness and try again.

_____

_____

_____

_____

Bent, Broken, and Cracked

The strongest of all warriors are these two—Time and Patience.
BASIL LIDDELL HART

1. After completing the airplane engine and getting their powered air machine to Kitty Hawk Island, the engine had one problem after another. Name two.

_____

_____

Kitty Hawk Island didn't have stores and factories like cities in the early 1900s. Outside of a small fishing village, little was on the island.

2. As the Wright brothers struggled with problems, the other men building powered air machines got closer and closer to flying. In order to be first, the brothers could have cut corners, but once again patience caused them to do things right. Reread the chapter and find out who else finished their machines.

first? _____ second?_____

third? _____

3. Did either of the first two attempts to fly succeed?_____

STUCK? *Being first doesn't mean much if you fail at what you're doing.*

W H A T   T H E   B I B L E   S A Y S

Read Matthew 20:26–27
Whoever wants to become great among you
must be your servant,
and whoever wants to be first among you
must be your slave.

According to these verses, God doesn't want His people putting all of their energy into being first. How would He prefer your energy be used?

_____

_____

_____

I T ' S   Y O U R   T U R N

There is little doubt that the Wright brothers wanted to be the first to try powered flight, but that desire did not affect their relationship with each other or the quality of their work. As a result, they were not the first to try—but they were the first to succeed.

Is there an area in your life where the desire to be first or best has made you impatient? Tell God about that area and ask Him to forgive you.

_____

_____

_____

CHAPTER EIGHT

59-Second Success

*Genius is nothing
but a greater aptitude
for patience.*

GEORGES LECLERC DE BUFFON

1. What major weather problems did the Wright brothers face when they decided to fly on December 17, 1903?

_____

_____

2. Which brother flew the longer flight?

_____

3. How long was the famous, successful flight of Wilbur Wright?

_____

STUCK? *Reread the chapter title.*

W H A T   T H E   B I B L E   S A Y S

Read 2 Thessalonians 3:5
May the Lord direct your hearts to God's love
and Christ's endurance.

Think about Christ's life: He was born in a stable, had parents who didn't understand Him, had disciples who made repeated mistakes, died on the cross, and had many people reject Him. Why do you think Paul prayed that the Christians in Thessalonica would have patience like Christ?

_____

_____

_____

I T ' S   Y O U R   T U R N

One last time, look at your waiting list in chapter 1. Now look at Christ's list above. Don't dismiss the differences by saying, "Yeah, but He's God." For thirty-three years Jesus limited Himself to being a man. He does understand what it is like to be young and have to wait.

In prayer, give the things on your list to Jesus Christ. He understands that patience isn't easy.

_____

_____

_____

_____

Activities

From Ground to Air with the Wright Brothers

Earn Your Wings

In the Wright Brothers' Flight Competition!

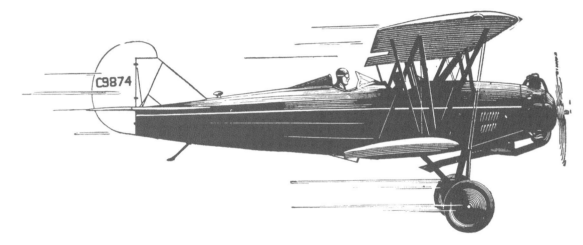

The American Wright Company is offering flight wings to young people who show superior endurance and ability by completing the books, finishing the flight experiments, and solving the puzzles in the activities section.

If you would like to take part in this competition, follow these instructions. Answer the question in each puzzle box throughout the book. Under some of the letters in the answer are small numbers. Take the letter from that space and place it in the proper blank on the last page of this book. When every space is filled, you will have solved the final puzzle, and you'll also have earned your honorary flight wings.

Example:

Clue answer D A Y T O N , O H I O
                    10   4

Back page _ _ _ H _ _ _ _ _ Y
           1 2 3 4 5 6 7 8 9 10

Imagining Flight

For thousands of years people have watched the birds and dreamed of flying.

What would it be like to sail above a city, a farm, a mountain, they wondered. Why couldn't they sail through the sky as well? It was a puzzle that great minds struggled with from China in the east to the United States in the west.

W hat is the name of one of the paintings that Da Vinci painted? To learn the answer, look in the "Did You Know?" section of this book. Fill in the blanks and copy numbered letters on the last page.

— — — — — — — — — — —
       3   6

Crazy Contraptions
Foolhardy but courageous, early inventors tried all kinds of crazy contraptions in their attempt to defy gravity. Jumping from towers or high cliffs to test their inventions, they fell, breaking their legs or their skulls.

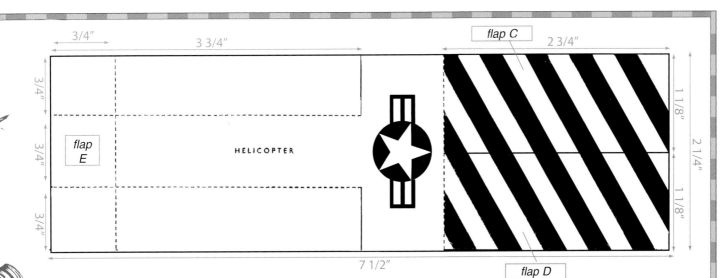

3/4" 3 3/4" flap C 2 3/4"

3/4"

3/4"

flap E

HELICOPTER

3/4"

3/4"

1 1/8"

2 1/4"

1 1/8"

7 1/2"

flap D

Leonardo da Vinci

Leonardo da Vinci, a gifted artist in the fifteenth century, thought a lot about flight. He designed flying machines with flapping wings. Though these didn't work, he understood some flight concepts hundreds of years ahead of others. He invented a four-cornered parachute and designed a type of helicopter with a spinning, screwlike propeller intended to make it rise into the air.

MAKE A HELICOPTER

NEEDED: *piece of paper, scissors, pencil, ruler*

DIRECTIONS:

1. Cut a piece of paper to measure 7 1/2" by 2 1/4". Using a pencil and ruler, divide it as shown above.
2. See illustration above as example. Using inch dimensions, draw solid and dotted lines to match on your rectangle.
3. Fold flap C toward you and flap D away from you. These are the rotors for your helicopter.
4. Now fold up the bottom, flap E, as shown in the illustration.
5. Stand on a chair, then reach high and drop your helicopter. It will fly.

How does it fly? The air under each rotor pushes it up. Since the rotors are bent in opposite directions, the air pushes them in opposite directions. This causes the helicopter to rotate as it falls.

Early Flight Efforts

The Chinese used kites to experiment with flight over two thousand years ago. But it wasn't until the 1700s that westerners tried flight. The first efforts involved different kinds of wings and parachutes. Then the hot air and hydrogen balloons were discovered. Lighter-than-air balloons flying caught the public imagination and became so popular that plates were painted with balloons, and toy balloons appeared in stores.

Balloooning

France led the way in ballooning. Two brothers, Joseph and Etienne Montgolfier, designed the first hot air balloon to fly with passengers in 1783. It flew for twenty-five minutes over Paris.

Ballooning became popular, and many people paid for balloon rides at fairs and carnivals. Later when Germans invaded France in the Franco-Prussian War, more than a hundred people escaped from Paris in balloons.

Gliding

Many people tried to glide from tall buildings, hills, or cliffs using various kinds of wings or parachutes. Some lost their lives. One of these was Franz Reichelt, a tailor from Austria, who made silk wings. He strapped them on and jumped from the Eiffel Tower in Paris—190 feet above the ground! His wings failed and he fell to his death.

Today air travel is big business. What was the name of the first aircraft that transported passengers? You'll find it in the "Did You Know?" section of this book.

_ _ _ _ _ _ _
9   11

66

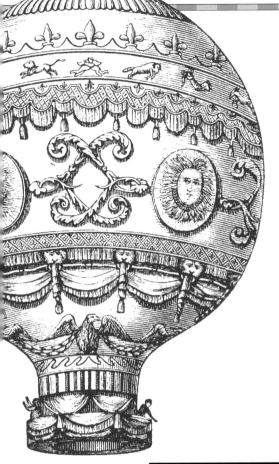

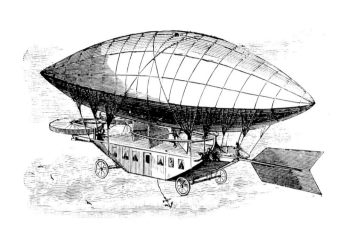

Dirigibles

Though people liked balloons, their flight had a problem. They could only go in the direction of the wind. Henri Giffard solved this problem by attaching a steam engine to a very large balloon in 1852. He flew it seventeen miles.

Later a Brazilian living in France, Alberto Santos-Dumont, built several dirigibles powered by gasoline engines. In 1901 he collected a 100,000-franc prize for flying his invention around the Eiffel Tower.

MAKE YOUR OWN PARACHUTE

NEEDED:

1 square of tissue paper (about 12 inches square)
4 pieces of thread (15 cm or 6 inches long)
cellophane tape
2 paper clips

DIRECTIONS:

1. Tape one thread to each corner of the tissue.
2. Tie together loose ends of thread in a knot.
3. Attach two paper clips near the knot to add weight.
4. Drop the parachute from the top of a porch or chair.
5. Experiment with different-sized parachutes.
6. Try cutting a hole in the center top of the tissue. (The air will escape evenly, giving a more gentle ride.)

Bird-Watching

Some flight enthusiasts thought that it was possible to fly heavier-than-air machines. Many of these early researchers studied birds and logically thought that a flying machine needed wings that flapped. After many failures, a few would-be fliers began to consider the flight of the hawk and eagle. They soared through the air without flapping. Using this idea, men started to build fixed-wing machines. The first ones had no engines and were called gliders.

The Wright brothers experimented with nonpowered wind flight before they tried flying a powered airship. What type of craft did they first fly at Kitty Hawk? You will find the answer on page 16.

— — — — — —
13   5

Otto Lilienthal

Otto Lilienthal studied soaring birds. He learned that it takes longer for the air to flow over the top of a bird wing (which is curved) than it does for the air to flow along the bottom of the wing (which is flat). The air on the top loses pressure because of the added distance, and the air on the bottom keeps its original pressure, pushing the wing upward. He called this "lift." Using the principle of lift, he designed gliders that worked!

In five years he glided more than two thousand times, but in 1896 he died in a glider crash.

EXPERIMENT WITH A WING

Build a wing and then make it fly by blowing "wind" on the front of it with a hair dryer.

NEEDED:

Spool of thread
Cellophane tape
One straw
Hair dryer
Piece of typing or computer paper
Scissors

DIRECTIONS:

1. Fold paper as shown, making one side about 2 cm or 3/4 inches smaller than the other.

2. Tape them together.

3. Punch a pencil through both sides of the paper wing to make two holes in the center (one above the other).

4. Cut the straw so it is long enough to go through the holes with a little extra sticking out on each side. Insert the straw through the wing holes.

5. Tape each side of the straw to the paper.

6. Slide a piece of the thread through the straw. Tie the thread to a weight of some kind and pull the top of the thread straight.

7. Use a hair dryer to blow air over the wing's curved top.

What's happening? The air travels faster over the top of the wing, causing the air pressure to drop. The higher air pressure underneath the wing pushes the wing up the string.

Octave Chanute

An American researcher, Octave Chanute, wrote about flight and encouraged others experimenting with it, including the Wright brothers. He designed a sixteen-foot biplane glider that tested well in 1896. The Wrights used some of Chanute's framework design in their first biplanes.

Octave Chanute

Flight Control

Blériot XI Monoplane
The first to fly across the English Channel on July 25, 1909.

Unlike most flyers of his day, Wilbur Wright believed that to maintain flight and avoid a crash, a pilot had to know how to control his aircraft. He figured this out by reading the writings of others who had studied flight and looking at previous flying information. For almost a year Wilbur and his brother Orville experimented with a handmade wind tunnel that tested the way different sizes and shapes of little wings flew.

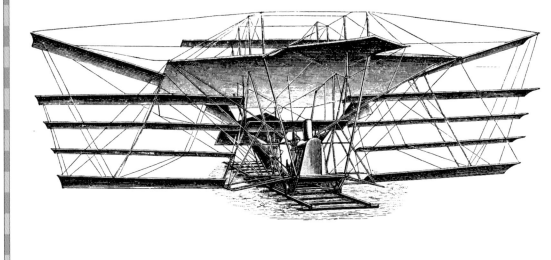

Maxim's Giant, 1894
Sir Hiram Stevens Maxim's enormous invention had a wingspan of 104 feet and weighed 3 1/2 tons. Despite its two 180-horsepower steam engines, it barely lifted off the ground.

His invention was not successful because it lacked the means for a controllable flight.

Three Types of Control

Wilbur and Orville learned that an airship pilot needed to control its movement in three directions:

Pitch *An airplane is pitching when its nose and tail go up or down.*

Yaw *When an airplane is yawing, it stays level but its wings swing to the right or left of the direction it is moving.*

Roll *An airplane rolls when its wing tips move up or down.*

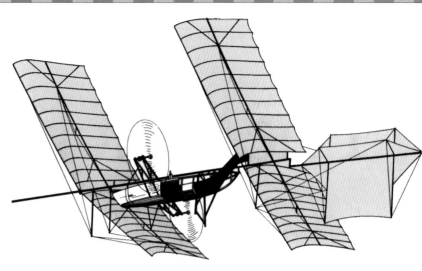

Professor Samuel Langley

About the time that the Wright brothers started work on a powered airship, Professor Samuel Langley, secretary of the Smithsonian, designed a craft he called an aerodrome. It was powered by a 52-horse-power engine. Before the Wrights flew their powered airship, Langley tried to launch his aerodrome from a track on top of a houseboat. His efforts failed twice, and the pilot had to be fished out of the water.

O n this page you have learned about the three different directions in which a pilot controls his plane. If a friend who owns a small plane flies toward your house and then turns left or right, what kind of movement is he using?

— — — — — —
8

Samuel Langley

The Wright Flyer

After years of study, experiments, and test flights with gliders, Wilbur and Orville made the world's first powered airplane flights near Kitty Hawk, North Carolina in 1903. They called their plane the *Flyer*. It measured twenty-one feet long and weighed a little over six hundred pounds without the pilot. The Flyer was smaller and more easily handled than Maxim's three-and-a-half ton *Giant* or Langley's seven-hundred-thirty pound *Aerodome*.

Orville Wright

Wilbur Wright

Propellers
The two propellers turned in opposite directions thrusting the Flyer forward.

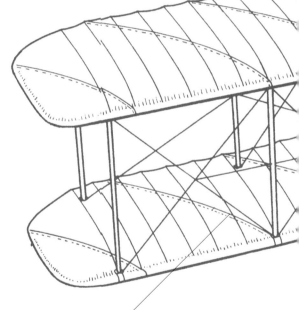

Wing-Warping Wire
Operated the warping (bending) of the wing tips in order to control rolling (side to side) motion.

Controlling the first airplane's flight wasn't easy! Wilbur and Orville had to make their hands, feet, and hips do separate actions at the same time. What part of the plane did they operate with their left hands?

— — — — — — —

7

Radiator
This water-filled radiator helped keep the engine from overheating.

Gasoline Tank
The gasoline tank held less than a half gallon of fuel. The Wrights estimated it was enough to fly for eighteen minutes.

Rudder
The rudder controlled the movement of the Flyer toward the right or left.

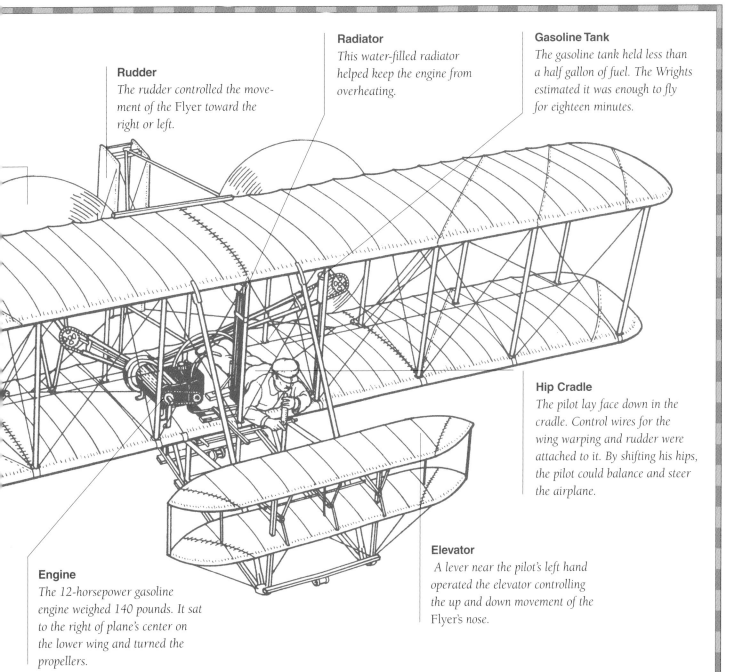

Hip Cradle
The pilot lay face down in the cradle. Control wires for the wing warping and rudder were attached to it. By shifting his hips, the pilot could balance and steer the airplane.

Engine
The 12-horsepower gasoline engine weighed 140 pounds. It sat to the right of plane's center on the lower wing and turned the propellers.

Elevator
A lever near the pilot's left hand operated the elevator controlling the up and down movement of the Flyer's nose.

Progress in Flight

World War I (1914–1918) and World War II (1941–1945) forced the United States to speed forward in designing fast airplanes that could travel at high altitudes, carry heavy loads, and go long distances without refueling. Manufacturers scrambled to meet these needs.

Soon after men started flying, women did too. But one African American woman was denied entrance into American flight schools. She ended up going to France to get her training. She became the first African-American woman pilot and did barnstorming to raise money to start a flight school for blacks. What was her name? You will find it on page 42.

14   4

P-51 Mustang
The P-51 Mustang was one of the best fighter planes of WWII. It could reach speeds of more than 400 mph, hit altitudes of twenty-five thousand feet, and travel more than two thousand miles without needing more fuel.

Curtiss JN-4 Jenny

At the beginning of WWI the United States only had fifteen airplanes compared to Germany's fifty-five! We raced to catch up, at first only using planes for watching behind enemy lines. But as German and American manufacturers worked on new planes, they soon started attaching machine guns for firing on enemy planes. Then bombs were added to drop on enemy positions and factories. The small biplane "Jenny" was the most common plane of the war.

After the war young pilots without jobs bought old warplanes and did stunt flying at fairs and carnivals. This was called barnstorming. Often stuntmen would walk on the plane during flight or even climb from one airplane to a second. After the show people paid for airplane rides.

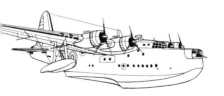

Short S.25 Sunderland III, 1942
This British seaplane was called Porcupine because of its heavy armament.

Avro Lancater B.I., 1944
This British heavy bomber flew the first bombing mission into Germany.

Henschel Hs 123-1, 1939
Used by Germany during the Spanish Civil War as a dive bomber.

Courageous Flyers

After the Wrights' successes, flying continued to catch the imagination of courageous young men and women. Everyone wanted to be the first to succeed in some aspect of flying—to fly further, at a higher speed, or at a higher altitude than anyone else.

Charles Lindbergh
The first solo flight across the Atlantic Ocean was made by Charles Lindbergh in 1927. He flew a single-engine monoplane, The Spirit of St. Louis, *from New York to Paris in 33 hours 32 minutes.*

The Ninety-Nines Club sponsors many educational and safety programs. What is the name of the annual flying award that it presents? Look in the "Did You Know?" section of this book to find it.

_ _ _ _ _ _ _ _ _ _ _ _ _ _
1   10

_ _ _ _ _

Harriet Quimby

A popular New York theater critic, Harriet Quimby enrolled in flight school in 1910. The next year she received her aviation license, becoming the first woman flyer in the United States.

Chuck Yeager

On October 14, 1947, Chuck Yeager became the first person to fly faster than the speed of sound. At an altitude of 40,000 feet, he pushed his X-1 to 662 mph. Eight years later, he used an X-1A rocket plane to fly more than 1600 mph! A near-death accident ended his test flying days. However, in 1997 at the age of seventy-four, he reflew his sound-barrier-breaking flight in honor of its fiftieth anniversary.

Amelia Earhart

In 1932 Amelia Earhart became the first woman to fly alone across the Atlantic Ocean. She flew it in a record-making 13 hours 30 minutes. She was also the first woman to fly across the Pacific Ocean from Hawaii to California. Later in 1935 she made a record flight from Mexico to New York City in less than 15 hours. She lost her life while attempting to fly around the world.

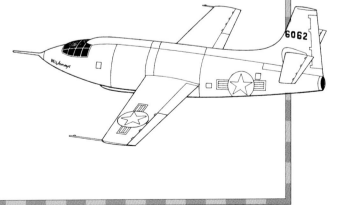

Today's Aircraft

Today thousands of airplanes take off from huge airports around our country. People think nothing of flying from Los Angeles to New York City in only six hours.

Air travel is so common that planes follow regular highways in the sky. Some people even own their own small airplanes for business and pleasure. And now we even have rockets that soar to Mars. Perhaps one day flying machines will take us to distant locations in our universe!

Today's U.S. Navy maintains a team of stunt flyers called the Blue Angels. Based on the information on this page, what kind of planes do you think they fly?

_ _ _ _   _ _ _ _ _
2

_ _ _ _ _ _
12

Apache Attack Helicopter

The Apache is the most advanced helicopter gunship flying today and was designed to complement armored weapon systems on the battlefield. It is powered by two 1600-horsepower engines which give it a speed of nearly 200 mph.

EXPERIMENTING WITH JET POWER

NEEDED:

String or thread
Tape
Drinking straw, cut 4" long
Balloon

DIRECTIONS:

1. Thread a long piece of string through the straw.

2. Tie the thread between two chairs about six feet apart.

3. Lay a piece of tape across the straw near each end.

4. Blow up the balloon

5. Hold the balloon tight as you attach it to the straw with tape

6. Let go of the balloon and watch how jet power works.

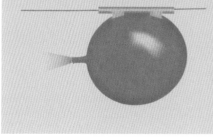

F/A-18 Hornet

The supersonic F-18 fighter plane is the nation's first strike-fighter. During Operation Desert Storm, F-18s shot down enemy fighters and bombed targets on the same mission.

The Hornet represents a major advance in aircraft technology. Reliability, maintainability, and survivability are all primary design factors that contribute to the lifespan of the Hornet. It could take a direct hit from an enemy missile, return to base, be repaired, and fly another mission the next day. The cockpit utilizes a sophisticated heads-up display to convey vital flight information to the pilot.

Airplane Industry

After the Wright brothers flew at Kitty Hawk, for five years they had a hard time selling their airplanes. Not so today! In 1994 the American aeronautic industry sold more than $100 billion in products and employed more than a million people. Aircraft are our country's top export to other countries, bringing in $40 billion each year!

American Wright Company

In 1904 the Wright Brothers put the cycle shop into Charlie Taylor's hands and gave all their time to building and flying airplanes. Five years later their flying business became the American Wright Company, a corporation. The head of U.S. Steel, the heads of Packard Motor Car Company, the owner of *Collier's Weekly,* and Cornelius Vanderbilt were a few of the investors who bought shares in the brothers' airplane company. After Wilbur died, Orville decided he liked being a researcher, not a businessman, and sold his shares.

Anemometer

This device measures wind speed. The most common anemometers have three or four "spokes" coming out from a center rod. At the end of each spoke, a cup is attached sideways to "catch" the wind. As the wind gets caught in the cups, it spins the center rod. The number of turns the rod makes each minute is used to determine the wind's speed.

Auto Racing

Early automobiles in the late 1800s were always breaking down. Only a few people bought them and often they were told "to get a horse" instead. Auto makers such as Henry Ford knew the public attitude toward cars had to change before people would begin buying a lot of them. So Ford and other manufacturers started racing their cars as a way to spark public interest. In many races, Ford won because his car was one of the few that didn't break down. Speeds in these early races sometimes reached more than 50 mph. Today race drivers travel at more than 200 mph!

Wilbur Wright

Aviatrix

In the early days of flying, a woman who piloted airplanes was given this name, the feminine version of aviator. In 1929 only ninety-nine women had pilot's licenses, but today thousands of women do. They fly commercial airplanes, military jets and helicopters, and even space shuttles.

Octave Chanute

This bridge builder didn't get involved with flying until almost his sixtieth birthday! He was an excellent engineer and was asked to write a series of articles on the development of flying machines. Chanute dived into the job, gathering information from every person he could find who'd worked on flying. Soon he was considered the world's best source of flight information. Though he never flew even a glider, he helped younger men do so, and the Wright brothers enjoyed his friendship throughout their flying years.

Did you

Amelia Earhart

In 1932 noted aviatrix Amelia Earhart became the first woman to fly across the Atlantic Ocean. Three years later she was the first woman to fly across the Pacific Ocean, and she broke the flight speed record from Mexico City to New York City. In 1937 she attempted to fly around the world. During the flight, she and her plane disappeared and to this day no one knows exactly what happened to it.

Barnstorming

From 1910 to the late 1920s, this term referred to the air exhibitions put on by daredevil pilots over farmlands. Before the Wright brothers' plane business was a success, Wilbur and Orville earned money by training pilots and putting on air shows. As the stunts got more spectacular, many pilots crashed, including some of the Wrights' trainees. By late 1911, the brothers had left this dangerous way of earning money.

Ritchel's foot-powered airship built in 1878 shows an early attempt to apply power to a balloon.

Everything You Ever Wanted to Know about the Time of the Wright Brothers

know?

but they crashed easily and in 1880 the "safety" bicycle appeared with both wheels the same size. The Wright brothers got into the bicycle business after chains, gears, and sprockets were added.

Leonnardo da Vinci

This Italian artist is best known for painting such classics as *The Mona Lisa* and *The Last Supper.* But Leonardo also studied math and physics. He was fascinated by the flight of birds and eventually sketched many flying machines. Two of his ideas, the propeller and the parachute, became important inventions centuries later.

Flying Fascination

Besides the people mentioned in *From Ground to Air with the Wright Brothers,* many other famous people studied and wrote about flying. Two of these were Alexander Graham Bell, who invented the telephone, and Thomas Edison, who invented the electric lightbulb.

First Airplane

The Wright brothers' original 1903 airplane was first preserved in the Science Museum of London. Later Orville gave it to the Smithsonian Institute in Washington, D.C. Full-scale copies of the Wright brothers' first airplane are also on display around the United States. One is at the Air Museum in Tucson, AZ. Looking at the plane's wood frame, wire supports, and canvas wings help a person realize the courage it took to go up in the air in such a flimsy machine.

to less than one hundred minutes. It lowered the cost of autos so more people could buy them.

Henry Ford also manufactured airplanes for awhile, his Ford Tri-Motor becoming an early mainstay in commercial aviation. It had three powerful 200-hp radial engines.

Hot Air Balloons

Two French brothers launched the first hot air balloon in 1873. But it was François Pilatre de Rozier who climbed into a basket to become the first person to fly in a lighter-than-air craft. But like all flying experiments it was dangerous. In 1875 de Rozier died when the gases in his balloon exploded.

Internal Combustion Engine

Gottlieb Daimler changed the automobile industry forever when he patented this new engine in 1887. Unlike the steam engine, it allowed for added speed without added

The Ford Tri-Motor Tin Goose carried 11 to 14 passengers seated in wicker chairs.

weight. Another inventor also did a lot of work with these engines about the same time Daimler did. His name was Karl Benz and in time his engines would be in automobiles called Mercedes-Benz.

Bicycles

Two-wheel vehicles called "hobby horses" showed up as early as 1690, but people had to push them with their feet to make them go. It wasn't until 1839 that pedals and cranks were added and riders finally got their feet off the ground. The first such vehicles were called velocipedes and were made of wood with iron wheels. They got the nickname "boneshakers." The term "bicycle" first appeared in 1869 after an Englishman put rubber tires on steel rims. High-wheel bicycles followed,

Gliders

Gliders are heavier-than-air crafts that do not have power engines yet are able to fly because of their bird-like shape. Lilienthal, Chanute, and the Wright brothers developed the long, narrow wings and measurements that enabled the glider to fly. After World War I, gliders were greatly improved in Germany. As the losers in the war, Germans were no longer permitted to have powered aircraft. In response they learned how to make bigger and better gliders for military purposes.

Henry Ford

Few people know that Henry Ford raced automobiles. He is best remembered for mass producing cars by using conveyer belts that carried the basic frame of an auto along to workers who added parts. This method cut the time it took to build a car from one and a half days

Orville Wright

Kitty Hawk

Along the North Carolina coast, an arm of the ocean cuts into the land. This arm of water is called the Albemarle Sound. Roanoke Island is near the mouth of the sound and beyond this larger island are scattered islands and marshlands called the Outer Banks. The village of Kitty Hawk is located on the Outer Banks near an area of large, open sand dunes that Orville once said he imagined looked like the Sahara Desert. To get to Kitty Hawk, the brothers took a train to Elizabeth City and then took a boat down the Pasquotank River, around Roanoke Island and to the Outer Banks.

Otto Lilienthal

This German glider pilot started the Wright brothers' fascination with flying. The articles they read about him while Orville had typhoid caused Wilbur to write letters to the Smithsonian and to Octave Chanute, asking about flying. Though this early flier died in 1896, Germany cast a bronze medal in his honor. It pictures Otto in flight on one side and his face on the other. It says, "The first human flight of the greatest teacher."

Charles Lindbergh

Lindbergh started flying in 1922 and went on to fly a mail run. In 1927 he decided to try for a twenty-five-thousand-dollar prize that required flying across the Atlantic Ocean without stopping. He made it in a small plane called *The Spirit of St. Louis*. This win made him the talk of Europe and America. Less than a month later he visited Orville Wright, who was excited to meet the new flying hero.

Math Confidence

More than one person has wondered why the Wright brothers decided to fly their plane in freezing weather and high winds, especially since Samuel Langley and Wilhelm Kress had recently crashed. Robert McCullough of Ferris State University in Michigan thinks he knows why the brothers went ahead with their plan. "I believe that the main reason for their confidence was mathematics." The figures recorded in the two brothers' papers show that they had a reasonable chance of success.

Ninety-Nines Club

This organization of women pilots started in 1929. Its name came from the ninety-nine women pilots who were the original members. Amelia Earhart was its first president, and it became famous for its cross-country flight race called the "Powder Puff Derby." The organization still exists today and it sponsors many educational and safety aviation programs. It gives an annual Katherine Wright Award (named for Wilbur and Orville's sister, whom they called "Kate") and keeps a great historical record of women fliers at their headquarters at the Will Rogers Airport in Oklahoma City.

1900 Olympics

While Wilbur and Orville were putting together their first man-carrying glider and trying it out at Kitty Hawk, the second Olympic games were being held in Paris. More than a thousand competitors from twenty-six countries tried for the gold medals, including nineteen women. The star of the 1900 games was an American named Alvin Kraenzlein, who won four gold medals in track and field events.

Orville's Crash

The Wrights got a contract with the army but had to prove that their plane could keep up a speed of 40 mph. They also had to train three army men to fly. Wilbur was in Europe, so Orville went to Fort Myer for the tests. He did well, flying every chance he got for two weeks and breaking records for length of time in the air. He took up an army observer and all went well until a propeller split on the fourteenth day of flying. Orville and the observer crashed. Orville had serious injuries and the other man died. Mechanical failure caused the tragedy.

Orville's Inventions

From childhood to old age, Orville loved to make things. When he was only twelve years old, he put together a makeshift printer and with Wilbur's help also made a lathe for shaping toys and gadgets. Later, after Wilbur's death, Orville went to work as a researcher. During World War I, he worked on a bomb with an attached engine that could fly on its own. It was called the Kettering Bug and showed great promise but the war ended before it was completed. It wasn't until World War II that guided missiles were developed and used.

Pluck and Luck

This magazine's flying adventures were the science fiction stories of the late 1800s and early 1900s. Some other well-known story magazines were *Frank Reade* and *Brave and Bold*. Many of these publications still exist today and are located in Colorado Springs, CO, at the U.S. Air Force Academy Library.

Smithsonian

This institution has the largest museum complex in the world. It keeps many of our national historical treasures and scientific collections. An act of Congress in 1846 started the institution and it's been going strong ever since. Today it has libraries containing 1.2 million volumes, sponsors research and exploration, and publishes books and pamphlets.

Teddy Bears

During the years that the Wright brothers worked on flying, fun things for kids appeared. Stuffed teddy bears named for President Theodore Roosevelt appeared in 1902 and Beatrix Potter's *The Tale of Peter Rabbit* first appeared in print in 1900.

The Tour de France cross-country bicycle race.

In the late 1940s an antibiotic was discovered that successfully treated the typhoid bacteria.

Telegram Mistakes

The telegram (a reproduction is enclosed in your kit) that was sent from Kitty Hawk on the day that the Wright brothers first flew had two mistakes in it. First it said the flight lasted only fifty-seven seconds, instead of fifty-nine. And it spelled Orville's name "Orevelle."

Tour de France

This race began in 1903 and is still going strong. In 2006 the race was more than 2,200 miles long instead of 1,500. One hundred and thirty-nine cyclists took part, using bicycles that had to weigh at least 14.998 pounds. Floyd Landis of the United States won the 2006 race and earned 450,000 euros.

Typhoid

This serious disease is caused by drinking unclean water or milk. It lasts many weeks, producing high fevers, chills, vomiting, headache, and sometimes internal bleeding. In the later 1940s an antibiotic was discovered that successfully treated the typhoid bacteria. But typhoid has almost disappeared in America due to the careful treatment of water and milk sources.

Victory Celebration

It wasn't until 1909 that Americans recognized the Wright brothers as the inventors of powered flight. When Wilbur, Orville, and Katherine returned from a successful trip to Europe, they were met in Dayton by ten thousand cheering people. Chinese lanterns, electric lights, a parade and huge banquet filled the next two days of celebrating. Dayton and the state of Ohio also made medals to honor the brothers.

World War I

This war took place from 1914 to 1918 and boosted the aeronautics industry. Both airplanes and lighter-than-air crafts were used for observation, attack, pursuit, bombing, and other specialized purposes. More planes were built and more pilots were trained during the war's four years than in the eleven previous years combined.

Wright Brothers Day

Congress designated December 17 of each year as "Wright Brothers Day" and requested that the President invite the people of the United States "to observe the day with appropriate ceremonies and activities."

Wright Family

Wilbur and Orville belonged to a close-knit family that included five children. Besides Katherine and Lorine, Wilbur and Orville also had an older brother named Reuchlin. Their father, Milton Wright, was a bishop in the United Brethren Church and he encouraged his sons in their experiments. Their mother died of tuberculosis when Wilbur and Orville were only twenty-two and eighteen years old.

The Dr-I Triplane was one of the most maneuverable fighter planes of World War I. It was one of the planes flown by German flying ace Manfred von Richthofen, "The Red Baron."

Zeppelins

The man-carrying balloons created by Count Zeppelin became the first aircraft used for commercial air service for passengers. They were also used during World War I for German air raids but were easily damaged by antiaircraft fire. After the war they went back to being passenger aircraft and did well until 1937 when a Zeppelin called the Hindenberg caught fire and thirty-six people were killed.

Earn Your Wings!

Now that you've completed this activity book, only one step remains in order to get your honorary flight wings. Using all the clues you've gathered in this book, see if you can name the specific place on Kitty Hawk Island where the Wright brothers first flew their airplane.

Fill in all the blanks below to discover the answer and earn your new honorary flight wings.

__ __ __ __   __ __ __ __ __   __ __ __ __ __
1   2   3   4   5   6   7   8   9   10 11 12 13 14

Congratulations!

You've shown superior endurance and ability by completing the flight experiments and solving the puzzles in this activity book. You've worked hard to earn your honorary flight wings!

Answers to clues: *The Last Supper, Zeppelin, Glider, Yawing, Elevator, Bessie Coleman, Katherine Wright Award, F/A-18 Fighter Planes.* Final Answer: *Kill Devil Hills.*